Where The Sun
Shines Best

ESSENTIAL POETS SERIES 200

Canada Council for the Arts

Conseil des Arts du Canada

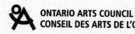

ONTARIO ARTS COUNCIL
CONSEIL DES ARTS DE L'ONTARIO

50 YEARS OF ONTARIO GOVERNMENT SUPPORT OF THE ARTS
50 ANS DE SOUTIEN DU GOUVERNEMENT DE L'ONTARIO AUX ARTS

Guernica Editions Inc. acknowledges the support
of the Canada Council for the Arts
and the Ontario Arts Council.
The Ontario Arts Council is an agency
of the Government of Ontario.

We acknowledge the financial support
of the Government of Canada through
the Canada Book Fund (CBF) for our publishing activities.

Where The Sun Shines Best

Austin Clarke

Austin Clarke

GUERNICA
TORONTO • BUFFALO • BERKELEY • LANCASTER (U.K.)
2013

Julie Roorda, editor
Michael Mirolla, general editor
David Moratto, interior designer
Guernica Editions Inc.
P.O. Box 117, Station P, Toronto (ON), Canada M5S 2S6
2250 Military Road, Tonawanda, N.Y. 14150-6000 U.S.A.

Distributors:
University of Toronto Press Distribution,
5201 Dufferin Street, Toronto (ON), Canada M3H 5T8
Gazelle Book Services, White Cross Mills, High Town, Lancaster LA1 4XS U.K.
Small Press Distribution, 1341 Seventh St., Berkeley, CA 94710-1409 U.S.A.

First edition.
Printed in Canada.

Legal Deposit – Third Quarter
Library of Congress Catalog Card Number: 2012953443

Library and Archives Canada Cataloguing in Publication

Clarke, Austin, 1934-
Where the sun shines best / Austin Clarke.

(Essential poets series ; 200)
Poems.
Also issued in electronic format.
ISBN 978-1-55071-693-1

I. Title. II. Series: Essential poets ; 200

PS8505.L38W54 2013   C811'.54   C2012-907650-3

For Gladys Irene Jordan Clarke-Luke, My Mother. 1914–2005

THE YELLOW leaves are trampled over by the black
boots of three soldiers from the Moss Park Armouries;
in uniform, intended not to be seen, nor identified,
for their intention and profession is to kill
to shoot from a distance, clean and perfect
and wipe their minds clean, erase all imperfection
of marksmanship. War. War has been declared.
War. It is all that's on their minds. War;
and the intention for war declared upon Moss Park.

Austin Clarke

THERE ARE three other men standing as if at attention,
though they are no soldiers; one man's posture is stooped
with old age, another is hampered by Saint Vitus' Dance,
uncertain in his balance and his gait,
all three men, crippled civilians, taking puffs from one
cigarette, from hand to lip, smoking their jewel of luck
found amongst the rotting cold leaves that numb
their fingers. A cough drop will clear their lungs,
after each passed puff, will make them high, will turn Canada
into Florida jaunty and warm, for five minutes, the life
of their happiness, and clear the head, to unlock the lungs
and watch the pure white smoke rise over their heads,
precious as the breath they breathe in this crisp December cold.

THEY ARE passing the stub, passing it, standing
under the bodies of maples and the other trees,
their names not taught in geography classes in Barbados.
They were not names learned by rote and heart, carried
here to this wide country of snow and wind and whiteness,
to take pause on their daily long journey, their constitutional,
in Moss Park, common in its uses, and users, not always swept;
condoms, discharged bullet-casings decorating,
in silent boasts of manhood, the shooting of anger,
desire, hunger after the flesh of women,
cheaper rates now that they are east of Jarvis, east of Church
and McGill, the prices lower the farther east you go.

Austin Clarke

I HAVE walked on these artificial, rolled-up leaves,
long-lasting and long out-living the fall of foot and instep,
flowers of cream plastic, a patch of two red ones,
boasting virulence in a man who has lasted longer
than the red and yellow fallen leaves from the trees
whose names I do not remember.

SQUEEZING THE last puff of joy from the joint
disappearing like spit on the lips, they move like soldiers
in disarray, shaken by the battle, ragged,
marching, "Easy!", coming in my direction.
I can see the last spit of marijuana cigarette
leave the lips of the man walking in fits,
alcohol and broken legs that barely balance him, who laughs
and jogs and plays like a doll sculpted from the two
stick-spines of a popsicle. He spits a smouldering last blob
of phlegm from deep inside his chest and walks
in a straight line, leading his two companions,
dragging his feet in the thick dying leaves.

Austin Clarke

THE LEAVES make the same sound as the poisonous dried
black pods of the shack-shack tree in an un-tilled field
in Barbados. His head is cut off, beheaded suddenly
by my window that is too small to frame his shoulders.
No rhythm to their footsteps as they walk like three men on stilts.
And I stand and think of popsicles and of men made of cloth
dropped from the needle-worker's sewing machine. And I think
of walking in the burning sun in Old Havana,
in a square, the playground of dictators; once; now an ordinary
square for tourists and the poor and prostitutes; turned
into a museum of contemporary knick-knacks and dolls,
piece-work for Cuba's poor and indigent, the works
of artists, and the frustrations of poverty: row after row
of golliwogs that stare me in the face, locked eyes of brotherhood,
and womanhood. I am embarrassed by my pity, as the whores
are following me, sticking to my black skin, like leeches,
like moles sucking the pity out of my Yankee dollar bills.

MOSS PARK Armouries where men just past puberty wait,
their heads buried in the silken pages of the Holy Bible,
praying for the luck of the draw and the trigger, to return
to this park. They come from the ticky-tacky suburbs
where identical and monotonous backyards clean as Pyrex bowls
after cornflakes, raked clean as skeletons, as if from plague
and household germs, and the influenza from pigs,
and bacon at the same hour of suspended morning.

Austin Clarke

YOUNG MEN waiting for the jet plane to Afghanistan
where poppies are pure and stronger, from Scarborough,
Mississauga, Don Mills and Brampton and condominiums
in Pickering, are certain of victory: for luck in war
is vouchsafed in beliefs, and luck of the dice, the presumption
that race and place, country and flag, give easier growth
to ego and hatred of men, and women, homeless and whores
who sleep on leaves the colour of gold, on a park bench cold
and damp, under a yellow sleeping bag, colder than raccoons
and squirrels warm in roofs and attics where they bury
tomorrow's breakfast and food for the week.

A MAN without a home, and a whore without a trick left
in her cold skirt, lie on two benches of cement
and wrought iron, a half-empty plastic cup of ants
that frolic on the surface leaving their journey marked
like lines in the middle of the palm, their horoscopes. They
    foretell
the beginning of dreams, of warmth, prosperity once known
and lived: the man was an editor, and printed stories
of homeless men; the woman remembers days
when her bed was warm with the body of a man beside,
her husband.

Austin Clarke

THREE SOLDIERS in uniform of dark green camouflage,
one with three stripes, one with two stripes, the third with
   one stripe
against him; their weapons left behind in a rack
in the Armouries with bigger guns, automatic, to kill in the dark,
and you don't know you're dead when you are dead.
These soldiers walk like the other three men who had left
the park before, puffed with pot, puffed with power.

THREE SOLDIERS, unsteady on their legs, stagger in
     uneven step
from the bar on Barton Street, where books of Canadian
     fiction once
were born; round the corner, walking-distance
from the Armouries. They are spinning and slipping-and-sliding
from blowing froth from the heads of draughts—more
than they could count—Canadian Molson's and U.S.
Budweiser, coming out on George Street dark as a back
alley, desolate patch of road a few steps down
from the Mission House which kisses Queen Street East.
They cross this road singing their favourite march,
"It's a long way to Tipperary," as the streetcars rumble; and they
imagine Kandahar, Afghanistan, and Canada's enemies.

Austin Clarke

Their arms become machine guns, and bullets fall
out of their mouths like a stream of bulbs on a Christmas tree,
    rapid;
repeating a long line of perfect aim.

They come upon the enemy: the man sleeping,
the camouflage of dark and yellow leaves covering
his body not exposed under the umbrella of the night, still,
    breathing
in the perfection of this black night, happiness
and fatigue gained from his collection of four empty bottles
drained to celebrate, and five cigarettes butted to one inch
of their life. "Let's scare the shit outta this fucker!
Trespassing on our Armouries! Bringing their shit ..."
The first attempt missed. The sole of his boot was wet,
and it hit the cement, and fell harmless; as the pain whizzed
through his ankle he lost his balance, and fell in the wet
freshly-cut grass. "Get-the-fuck off! Fuckers!"
the soldiers hissed, words boiling over like milk
in an enamel saucepan, like spit rising in small bubbles
in the fresh snow, like baseballs thrown at deadly speed
in the nearby empty diamond.

Austin Clarke

THE SOLDIER with three stripes on his shoulder ignores
        the woman
at Jarvis and Queen, mistaking her limber body for a back-pack
under a blanket in the half-darkness, in his hurry and his anger
to land his boots, left and right in the same soft spot on the man's
chest. She thought she could pull a trick on this night, safe
on the mowed lawn tucked neat inside the rectangle of fence,
blackened iron to protect the Armouries from invading whores;
attacking bloody beggars who cross the Rubicon,
brown dying grass carved into paths of Xs,
going and coming during the light of day and the unsafe
darkness of night, asking for spare change.

WHEN THE sun has left the skies, and stars come out
like fugitives, you can catch them swapping their bodies for
    a street-
car ticket to ride to the bars on Dundas Street,
to wash down the peckishness in a glass of draught beer,
in the same bar as the three soldiers, or a cup of coffee
getting thicker and colder, held with two fingers, as if
it is champagne, the same plastic cup I see them use
as an ashtray then drop into the uncollected green garbage bins
in front of my neighbour's house, the neighbourhood dump.

Austin Clarke

"DIRTY FUCKING shit! You fucker! How dare you
trespass on these Armouries?" And then, in the same blackness
of the night, he realized there were two sleeping bodies;
three fuckers fucking with the Armouries, noticing
the second body in the darkness, he screamed as if
it was this ghost that frightened him. "Fuckers!"
"Fuck-off!" the second soldier screamed, finding voice
and bravery in the blackness of the night. There were no walkers
of dogs peeing against a tree, just the ghosts in the shapes
of maples; just the wail of a police cruiser going in the wrong
direction; just the shriek of an ambulance. It was a shooting
on Shuter. A black man. Gang-related. Related.
It was a gangster sixteen years old, too young,
the Law said, to show the city his face, for only his mother
shall know, and his father, if there is a father living,
that he is dead. "Deading," as they say back where he originated.

"FUCK OFF!" he says, for no words suit the venom
in his body, only two hisses like daggers. "Fuck off!"
And the third man, without the anger to match his manhood,
to clothe his manhood in, stands silent. He turns
his face aside and says, "Pardon me," and the next
second all three are listening to a sound like water
hitting the ground pounding, pounding heavy as iron.
The sound of gushing water that could never rouse
the homeless man from his dream.

Austin Clarke

MOLSON'S DRAUGHT beer gurgling in his head, losing
his balance, he led his two companions tied by the rope
of friendship, members of the same cult and secret society,
a brigade of violence, tied to obedience in the same drills
of precision, standing at attention, "Left turn, right turn,
Roy-yal Sal-lute ... Pre-sent ... Ho!" the training manual
gave the words and drills, to inject bravery into the veins,
to squeeze bravery into violent vengeance mixed
with the corpuscles already there, floating in the weakened
red liquid that has turned pink.

"O, MARY, mother of God, I put my life into your two hands!"
"In the name of the Father, and the Son, and the Holy Ghost,
I entrust my life!" And the haunting voice spreads
the hoarse comfort of the blues, "Bring back, bring back,
bring back my bonnie to me, to me ..." without weapons
tied to their thighs, with no hand grenade, small
as a pineapple rotting on the stem, the size of a testicle,
manhood shrivels to the size of the balls of the sleeping man.

Austin Clarke

WITHOUT GUNS and hand-grenades, wearing their
    mufti-clothes,
blue jeans, blue t-shirt and black leather-and-canvas boots
tipped in steel, they came like sneaks upon the man
chloroformed in sleep, hard concrete for bed springs and
    bed bugs
from the halfway house. But the soldiers' words are bullets,
the cold steel of drawn bayonets stern as the iron
painted black on three sides of the Armouries, and keep
this homeless man from dreaming that the concrete of the park
bench is a soft made-up bed, enticing as a mattress
standing on display in a show window of a second-hand
store selling bayonets and goggles, swords and rifles,
helmets and boots from wars in foreign countries
the soldier could not find on a map of the world,
because he did not reach grade five in school, and was not
yet born when wars were fought and lost, in foreign countries
painted red in The Times Atlas of the World;
no geography in his head.

SURROUNDING HIM is his silent audience; tongues
cut to the stump, silenced and dumbfounded, unable
to tell their opinions, so speechless they have become
witnesses of the spectacle, in the arena, sitting on cushions
softer than the yellow maple leaves broken at the spine
and the ruptured veins, behind thick curtain and white
plastic blinds matching the colour of the television screen
reflected on its white face, intolerant of the blackness outside;
from three floors above the leaves in townhouses patterned
after England, Victorian and Georgian; their windows sealed
against the cold draught of the night, and the dust of summer,
to escape the smudge of life swirling around them,
as they fence themselves behind wrought iron, sturdy
as prison cells, in carbon copy of the barricade of iron
running round three sides of the Armouries to keep bums
and the sex-workers and homeless men hiding beneath heaps
of maple leaves rotting side by side with used condoms,
cigarette butts and chewing gum.

Austin Clarke

I STAND in this silence; in these shadows thrown from the
    Armouries
and the cannon sweating in the silent dew, coming alive
in the purr of this soldier's anger and fantasy; this cold
morning with the sun breaking in a soft cool kiss, a mist,
a cloud, weak enough to raise an aura from the dew on iron.
I hear the language that bathes his quarry clean,
words flung at the man without a home,
to wake him from his wet cold blanket; I sit,
try to stand, and count the number of times
the pendulum of the boot takes aim and lands in the stomach
of the sleeping man.

THE FLAG of Ontario, its Crown, its Cross of St. George,
three branches, from the maples in the park, and the trillium
     flower,
once silk and white, delicate and sensual,
covered in myth and superstition, not to be touched,
flies regal from my neighbour's second floor
window, guarding her roof, flapping in four
different kinds of wind in hurricane, storm and flood
and pouring rain that makes me think of Barbados,
fifty years ago, when the chattel house made from grey
unpainted deal board and sheets of galvanized tin
the colour of the skies when rain is falling, and the coral stone
were dumped in backyards, by the side of the road, hidden
in the gutters and cane fields, and the population bathed
in tears of blood, cried "Help!"; saw Sodom and Gomorrah,
moaning "Help we, O Lord, O Jesus Christ! Help we!"

Austin Clarke

THERE IS no sign of the three men smoking under the maples
in this morning's bright sun, now that the leaves have changed
from gold to brown and some have turned to garbage
irrefutable as condoms, and all of a sudden, I am not here,
    not here
across from the Park, where three nights ago, passing into
    morning
the three soldiers, sergeant, corporal and private
bound for Kandahar, Afghanistan and places drawn on maps
beat the brains clean out of the head of a homeless man
asleep in a bag on a cold concrete bench,
and counted the blows delivered with their polished black boots
with tips of steel which turned his statue to red liquid
the colour of blood when the sun rose, too late
for a safer bed, too early for Salvation Army breakfast.
Dead. When this same sun came up and showed him dead,
there was no light, no explanation, no motive
for the sport of blood, dripping down from the cement bench
speckled in red dots with tails attached,
illustrating motion, flight and escape.

THE MORNING cold sun shows only the slow long line,
women with their heads tied in black silk, concealing the length
of hair, the colour of eyes and lips. Robes
in many colours, of blue, and black, maroon, and dark-red,
flow on the brown grass, as mothers push prams and strollers
with infants in them who do not talk, who do not know
the meaning of this tragic silence, who are silent in their safety,
and do not cry or scream for joy as they swing
into the heavens of the blue skies.

Austin Clarke

WHO DO not cry, for they are dead to the violence of blood
marked by the rubber tires. Dead their mothers
push them to their daily care; and dead in sleep
they arrive: mother and child. In this clockwork obedience
with time and place they greet the baby-sitters drugged
in their own immigrant importance. These mothers push
the stroller and the pram with seldom help from men
who walk beside, on the safe side
from traffic, from mad men, and from policemen.

BUT THESE are obedient men, leaving the women
who mother their children and their tots, to live alone
and feel the full fragrance of the winds blowing cold
from the towers of the Royal Bank and other royal banks,
the towers of the Bank of Nova Scotia, Toronto Dominion,
the Trump Towers invading Toronto, and not a peddling bank
owned by a black man to give easy loans of two hundred
dollars to meet the rent, to meet the parking fine,
to re-establish dignity and manhood; the afternoon
his glee over-flowed thousands of others cheering the same
hope, and same fantasy, "Cahn lose! Cahn lose!
Not in this company! The other horses are donkeys!"

Austin Clarke

AT WOODBINE, and one minute later, a voice from the heavens
cried, "They're off!" Sharp and cruel as a sword
of lightning, and like lightning the voice chopped his hope
and his fantasy into smithereens, and all he could see
through the shards and the pieces of glass he mistook for crystals
and precious stones were the towers of banks, with no
dollar signs painted on them, and the yellow-painted recreation
centre, two storeys of ice rinks for men who do not want
to grow older than childhood before the puck is dropped.
They are left now, men in short pants, like boys, to face
the cement and the anger in the architecture of the Armouries,
and walk under the umbrellas of leaves of the Japanese maples,
investigate the slow moving water in the gutter,
hoping water can be made into wine in this Mount of Olives
barrenness, a man in a hurry to board a bus,
or a taxi, throws his burning American red-faced
Marlboros in the gutter, on my neighbour's lawn.

EARLIER YESTERDAY afternoon, there was a parade
of soldiers and officers, with spit, polish, bugles
and flash, trumpets marking the ceremony, bagpipes
wailing and drums beating in a slow death-march,
making you think there was a funeral, as if they knew
there would be a death.

Austin Clarke

WHEN THE first blow landed, the sound was muffled, covered,
concealed beneath the blanket of yellowing leaves,
and his marksmanship was like an arrow driven
into the hole made by the previous blow. The blow
caused by his comrade, born in Canada, enlisted to travel
through dust and storm, through plantations of fertile bush
and poppy excellent to inhale, from Afghanistan
to Shuter Street, they say.

THE THIRD companion-witness made a wish
that was a dream that he was not there that night to see
and hear, as witness and fool, that he was still back in the Island,
poor, black and hungry, wishing that luck and a smile
from the immigration officer would land him in the other
prison of Canada's racialism. "But not there, Y'Onner,
on the Friday night, in the park, when the sergeant
was kicking the man, mistaking the man for a terriss,
and he was behaving like he was in Afghanistan.
I only play baseball only in the park, as I watch the two o' them
kicking and shouting and calling out 'strikes'. Stop,
I screamed, stop, as my shouts matched the landing of the black
boots. Stop! Stop, I screamed. Stop.
But my shouts matched the landing boots upon the man's
chest, in matching rhythm with the landing blows. Stop!"

Austin Clarke

IT WAS a scream of horror, in a dream, for he was not,
could not be watching the same man he drank Molson's
    draught beer
with, man-for-man, Molson's-for-Molson's; he was not
in Afghanistan, was not killing Talibans, wasn't on patrol,
in the midnight blackness matching the colour of his own
skin, in that park, in this city, in this diamond.

IT WAS a nightmare; he was sleeping on a Serta mattress
under the sheets fresh from the washing machine,
up in the suburbs, Scarborough, Don Mills, Mississauga,
in comfort beneath the sheets ironed to perfection.
A dream: had to be, since his presence here in this country
as an immigrant working his way up, rank by rank,
job by job, night watchman, taxi driver, before he knew
the streets, was close to tumbling down.

Austin Clarke

HIS DREAMS are melting. He is not here in this park,
on this Friday, in this blackness of extinguished lights,
empty except for them, two Canadians and an immigrant;
a man kicked to death; a woman dialling in the darkness
holds her cellular phone to her frightened lips
and whispers into it, "Nine-one-one? Nine-one-one?"
into this black Friday. "Is this Nine-one-one? ... is ..."

THE HEAVENS blacken the immigrant soldier, burdened
by Christianity and hope on earth, and by his burial ground
when he is dead, opened with the glory of warm
sunshine the next day, Saturday, when the swings in the park
were aeroplanes, and Canada geese and seagulls
were the Spitfires and darts attacking the stale bread thrown
by bird-lovers on the hard ground, near the three small
    mountains
of leaves piled high and rotting near the community kitchen
garden gouged into the black soil mixed
with the rotted vegetables, where sunflowers grow high
as sweat under an immigrant's arms five-foot-five in height.

Austin Clarke

WOMEN FROM Somalia dressed all in white, heading to mosques
and Muslim prayers, their faces covered with masks
of fine white silk and black cotton, walk
on this unhallowed ground splattered with blood and death
and fallen maple leaves, on which there was a murder.
Last night's murder. And all the other homeless men,
already awake early now in the mild morning wind,
generous to the last man, building a brotherhood,
that talks in whispers, and with their eyes, since last
night's bloodletting, helping one another to reach
the linoleum on the large table spread for a last supper
of a cuppa coffee already cold, slice of toast
wet from the spread of margarine, limping on sore
feet, to beat the crawling crowd on both sidewalks,
to reach the table of Salvation Army breakfast first.

HERBS, FLOWERS, short trees that bear peas, vines
that hold tomatoes, cucumbers, and the tall faces of sunflower
the colour of fallen leaves in spring and in summer,
are now dead, and this is why there is no memorial
of flowers marking the scene of murder, the killing of a man
nameless before someone dug up his past and found
he was an editor, a man of words, silenced now,
unable to write his own obituary.

Austin Clarke

THERE ARE no cards of condolence, no memorial at any
of the three cathedrals that butt-and-bound the Moss Park
Armouries silent as the black wrought iron fence
that circles it, separating the home of the homeless, men
and women, on Queen Street East who stand and wait.
No one shall come by bus, train, aeroplane,
helicopter from the west, the home of the dead man
before he came hopeful, homeless to the east; no one to sing
his praise, to write a poem on his own violence,
gouging the words out of the fragile skin of his life,
mercifully unable to look backwards, onto his murder,
and give the correct punctuation to his narrative.

YOU ARE not the only one to feel the anger poverty breeds;
you are not the only one martyred with nails and kicks,
to the cross of savagery; you are not the only one raised
to glory on a cross, after your crucifixion, blessed
by the silence of raving crowds. On a blessed bier
of marble steps you walked up, counting four,
to reach your bed on the hard cement. One.
Two. Three. Reaching the fourth slab.
And when your feet landed safe,
landed safe in this lonely journey,
alone in the midnight safety you used to know,
Thursday, Friday, Saturday night, early Sunday morning
before the neighbourhood washed their faces and made
the sign of the cross with the same water, with the same
    hand, there,
on the fourth cement step, was where they found you.
You were already dead, in your sleep, beaten
to everlasting silence, everlasting death, leaves
to ashes, without clothes, naked as at your birth, above
the grave of the marble steps.

Austin Clarke

AND WHEN the Bishop found you before the morning mass,
he wrapped your death in the drops of holy water,
bathing you in holy proclamation
that you were not only "a child of God": you were,
he said, the modern-day Jesus Christ, in truth.
"This Lamb of God, we must worship this black Jesus."
And the congregations sang hymns of adoration and of love.
The sexton had already poured detergent, in more
generous drops than wine, where your body had lain,
making a sign of the cross, on the white marble steps.

IN ANOTHER country, far away from this Toronto cold,
in Italy, in Vicenza, where the swastika and the soaring eagles
escaped the demolition of Nazi architecture which still soars
like pigeons in the park, fighting for the guts,
fighting over the guts of animals
smaller than themselves, where they had captured Jews,
the new illegal citizens, undertakers, illegal
immigrants homeless out of Africa, who sleep on the steps
of this cathedral large as the main post office, large
as a castle, large as a villa for noblemen,
larger still than the Armouries in Moss Park.

Austin Clarke

HE WAS black before the fury of three soldiers
pointed out his nationality, and had him christened
as the black Messiah of immigrants. But the colour of his skin,
his blackness, is advertised throughout the world
in cities—London, and Amsterdam, Paris, richer
from his labour, but not enriched by his smell of his sweat.
His sweat was sold now by the pirates, explorers who discovered
him, where he was born and lived as an inhabitant,
they found him; and sold the fragrance of his smell,
to merchant ships. His smell was bottled into perfume
vials; smells that could not fumigate the stench
of his enslavement. Youth Dew, Chanel pour Monsieur,
Louis Philippe for Men, even No. 4711 Echt Kolnisch Wasser,
lost their strength. Pimp Oil remains now, strong
as the smell of a carcass mixed with the smell of slavery.

Where The Sun Shines Best

IN BROOKLYN and Harlem, N'Orleans and Halifax, London's
Notting Hill, Toronto's Moss Park, the suburban ghetto
of Malvern in the east, and Jane-Finch in the west,
bearing the blame for all iniquities of colour
where luck, good and bad, mostly bad,
placed him in the belly of the pig, in the bowels of the goat,
in the sewer of the bubbling intestines washed in lime juice,
the confidence of cleaning shit from limbs tottering on the brink
of the grave, turned inside out, and then funnelled, forced
through the white enamel ladle; boiled for hours
in superstitious silence.

Austin Clarke

AND HIS mastery with tails and guts and pig's snout
turned into a richer inedible thick brown soup;
to paste. And it followed him like a stream of lava, over
the volcanic rock of his journeys in the holds of merchant ships
lying in shit, faeces, amongst other deformed bodies
twisted in the tropical heat; crossing the Atlantic Ocean;
and when he landed in unknown ports, the different
languages, the thicker humidity, breathing now difficult,
disorientated, Bridgetown, Kingston, and Charleston,
Williamstadt, Curacao and Port-au-Prince and Halifax
from 1820 onwards.

WINGING JOURNEYS battling immigrants from hot
cotton to humid sugar cane, snake-infested, with whip
and rape memorialized in bronze statues and literature
that reproduced them as beasts, not only beasts, but niggers,
raised aloft on billboards, golliwogs to advertise
the finest in teas and Seville orange marmalades for English
appetites grown in the mid-day sun of India.

Austin Clarke

THESE THREE soldiers bound for the stifling dust
of Kandahar, one of them, the descendant of slaves,
was their "brother," their comrade-in-arms. In cowardice
he was joined to them, eventually employed to mark
that difference in his lot pulled out of a hat, not by his own
desire and wish, but scrawled upon his black skin,
in the fallen rotting leaves no longer bright
and yellow and shining clear in the patterns of Persian
and Afghan carpets too expensive for his small soldier's pittance
of a salary. He had chosen, or had volunteered, to travel miles
in cloud and dust from the yellowing maple leaves in a park,
in a Toronto neighbourhood so safe from the triggers of death.

DID HE ever think of his vantaged view from the nailed
wooden box, plain as a pauper's coffin as it rests
on the lip of a grave in one of the three cathedrals'
small marble tombs, graves similar to the busy Mount Pleasant
Cemetery on Yonge Street, in the hollow of the road, amongst
    thick
flowers and mowed grass, the marble headstones, miniature
    castles
and high-risen sky-scraping condominiums, castles too
lugubrious for death? Didn't he think of weeping mothers
like his own, recent from Africa, survivor of the crossing,
her memory crammed full of the creaking of ropes
in sails, monotonous as the thick green waves running
in the opposite direction, going back to Africa?
Her history of ships and running water, in holds
in which her body touched men, and was sprinkled by vomit,
and sex in the bowels and high-smelling entrails of that voyage?
That journey? She can remember the past: can fantasize no future.
Let her, in her new grief, therefore weep for your atonement.
And let her weep for hers.

Austin Clarke

WERE YOU so unprepared as were armies of soldiers in years
gone by, such a coward that you could not use your spear,
your javelin, your Uzi, or a piece of strong rope
to make a necklace with a reef knot, and adorn your bravery
with an act of suicide? Did they not teach you, in drills
and in mercy, the disdain to be captured alive by the enemy,
to do the noble thing, and take your own life?
Years ago, when men thought they were men, in the time
of Roman legions, that act of selfishness was accounted
more brave than to fall into the hands of the enemy. Fall
therefore, into the steps of honour, to carry out this sacrifice?
And die a man? You have, now, in that black night,
you have surrendered that manhood, been feathered
after you were tarred by history, made accessory before
and after the fact. What the fuck! The fact, I mean.
What is your fact of dignity?

AND NOW, we who wear the same uniform of brotherhood,
are left to mourn for your cowardice, unfit to be draped
in the Canadian flag, or the flag of Ontario, remembered
only as a murderer, for the thickness of blood running red
as the Maple Leaf. Was it as thick as the impulse to belong,
to be a brother? Or did you, in silence, become
merely white, thick, glue?

Austin Clarke

WE SHALL cover the kettle drum with black cloth,
and make the bagpipe pianissimo, to hear the lessening last breath
of a man without a pot to piss in, who lay beneath
the boots of the leader of your three-manned platoon.
Soft, soft, very soft shall the Maple Leaf blow in the winds
that comb the park, as it is lowered to half its dignity.
Soft shall be the cries of the unemployed,
the miracle workers selling the magic of sex;
for the piled decaying maple leaves shall stoke
no funeral pyre, no memorial shall be mourned;
"walkers" in your funeral shall obey
the silence of witnesses, the silence of guilt, the silence
of ignorance, the silence of the immorality that surrounds
the park leaving abandoned plastic wrappers of used
and misused condoms, cigarette stubs, Styrofoam cups
emptied in greed and hunger; two states of mind
that have no choice nor difference of luck.

Three men, one with caution in his step,
limbs jerking with his Saint Vitus' dancing steps;
the second one covered in a salt-and-pepper beard
that conceals his lips and changes the emotional landscape
of his face, hidden like the countenance of the women
shrouded in silk covering face and lips with slits
for eyes; the third man from India; make a trio of conspiracy,
boarding in the boarded-up house at the eastern end of the park,
painted grey, for tidiness; are now under the tree sealing
their friendship with the disappearing inch
of the forbidden cigarette. They cross the street
looking in the wrong direction, clouded by the strength
of the burning roach they throw into the pile of rotting leaves,
and when it touches the yellowing leaves there is no simmer,
no sound as from a frying pan with bacon on their two-
burner stove; when they look up in my direction, I
see only the top of their heads: balding, quivering
with the dance of Saint Vitus, the third man with a pile of
        grey covering
his pate like an old, stained rug the same
colour as the carpet in the home where they wipe leaves and shit,
from the frolicking dogs exercising in the park, and a single
used condom stuck to the white heel of the Adidas
of the man from India, who is accustomed
to sharing the street with cows unaccustomed to white
lines painted in the thoroughfare that divides the right-of-way
between man and beast, with his feet slapping the tar
without shoe or sandal, slapping the hot road, dodging
and bobbing-and-weaving from the brown steaming pancakes,
dropped with a sound of hollow certainty, and something
        like steam
rising from his lathered bare feet. Shit.

Austin Clarke

BUT THEY strolled away from me at my window two floors above
their heads, satisfied, dizzy from the shared cigarette
wrapped in brown shop paper for concealment from the uniform
in the police cruiser. The judgement was already made of these
three: bums, homeless bastards, "... before I throw
the three o' youse in a goddamn cell." Or, the cruiser could've run
them down; but there were too many witnesses, other
"homeless bas ..." Tires screeched high with speed
heading to the Division. Like a nail dragged across
a pane of glass.

THE NIGHT before, the soldiers counted the number of times
the cathedral bell signalled the time, striking clear and mournful
in the crisp night, measuring off midnight, and the quarter after
midnight; the square wooden table rocked with their weight
and their loss of balance, and six hands touched the glasses
and the cigarette butts and the spilled grains of salt, and the small
balls of chewing gum stuck to the cheap glass ashtrays,
one for each, and hard-boiled eggs in vinegar
that matched their tough appetite for beer, and three
shot-glasses empty, like three full-stops, that had held
Irish whiskey, punctuation marks to a night of celebration:
they were leaving next week, for Kandahar, so this was a night
to say farewell. They were drunk. Drunk from Molson's
and fear and stories of desert dust. Blang!
Blang! Buh-lang! The bells were singing goodbye.

Austin Clarke

THEY COULD see yards ahead of them, the three of them
    could count
cars parked on both sides of Britain Street, and read
their number plates, in the spaces cleared for condominium
and loft; and they looked up and saw lights on in an office
and in a townhouse, the three happy larks singing,
"It's a long way to Tipperary," slapping the back
of one on his green uniform, one after one, tight
in this triumvirate of brotherhood, pals on their way
to a camouflage theatre of war, to Afghanistan and dust
and the stuffing of cigarettes grown in thick profusion
in small towns not yet bombed by America, Great
Britain, Russia, and France, the world's great powers
who invented niggers, slaves, the prejudice of skin
and colour, and wogs, Amsterdam not excluded from this G-l0
society, buddies, sent the missionaries to discover
and convert the infidel for the last time, from a whisper
even a whisper of Allah, these new guns bring three new Bibles
hidden under their uniforms, instead of sticks of dynamite
taped to the heart, to civilize, "What the hell,
fuck up those terriss-bastards!"

THE THREE of them are camouflaged in green,
faces blackened to fool the enemy, resembling
Al Jolson pretending to be black in painted face
singing the blues of black people. But his body remains
white and his soul is buried in whiteface singing,
the dirty black blues: "Mammy," "My Ole Kentucky Home,"
and "Georgia." His voice is a black face of black chalk; but yours,
your face is indelible, and no eraser nor soap
can lighten the darkness of your bed. It is a short walk
from Britain Street, turn right, and come to George and
    Queen Street
East. They can see now, the hostel on their left hand,
for the work-less, home-less, man-less, husband-less men;
and women; and the four cannons are silent as the iron rail
    scrapped
from South Africa and the Boer War, before the three were born;
look left and look right, with drunken eyes that see
only in double; cross the street, and we're home!
The Armouries ... "Our Armouries! And this homeless bugger
is sleeping on our property? You don't belong here, fucker!
Go back to your home!"

Austin Clarke

STURDY IN concrete, iron fence wrought in apartheid,
black as a Maginot Line that separates men
who sleep on benches and men who sleep on canvas army cots
curtained in peaceful blackness when the lights are turned out,
it is quiet. The room in deep black imitating the colour
that Al Jolson chose to paint his face, to charm his audience,
to show love for a black voice. "Mammy, Mammy, Oh Mammy."
He was not thinking of the woman who buried his navel string
in the desert of his birth, in the caked land, in the dry desert,
in her memory; and here now, in this country with no history
of wars fought, or won or lost, on its land, she brought you,
for your safety, she spared you from the new fashion
of wearing bombs, instead of suspenders or a leather belt,
round your waist, five dollars, strapped to your ribs and legs.

AND NOW, she must stand in the packed court, and watch
the insults in the glance, in the stare, in the mannerism,
on the lips of your two new comrades-in-arms;
camouflaged in uniforms that place you plump in the scope
of your enemy the Taliban, undistinguished from a sprouting stalk
of poppy. Do they place a red, unreal poppy at the top
of their hearts, on Remembrance Day? And pin it in a button hole,
or your beret every day that falls on the eleventh of November?
Or, is it merely a verdant reminder, in its two-faced
agricultural importance sprouting from your uniform the colour
of light-brown sand that sends you back to Africa, or the
    Caribbean
and the pounding of drums fading into a buzz, like water
in the ear, throbbing like the sea, like waves going and coming?
You will remember Mogadishu.

Austin Clarke

NOW, IN sadness you must face the bloody book of Law,
when your Mother's touch is prohibited, her words of comfort
forbidden. The other defendants are flanked and two
surrounded, by mother, father, brother, sister,
sons and daughters, and the suburban up-scaled street
of condominiums identical along its lawns trimmed like the cut
of hair the army placed upon your head, like a rubber
    bathing cap.
You will hear your name and not know it is your name
that passed their lips, and your mother will sit in disbelief,
too deaf to hear the colour of the Law, the colour of blood
used to define you: "When the second boot landed in his chest,
the homeless man was already dead; his heart was no longer
    ticking;
not beating; foam like a squirt of cream settled at the corners
of his mouth, yes? The convulsions of his body were not
able to brush it off? Blood came from his mouth? Yes?"

THE JUDGE had pity on you. He looked into your mother's face,
counted the drops of tears, jewels in her eyes,
read the plea he saw in them, her silent words that broke his heart.
A woman, in terror like your Mother, had whispered nine-one-one
into a cellular phone, like a conspiracy. "They're killing him!"
she said, smothering her voice, as if she was the victim,
but knowing that she, married to him in danger, could be next.
"Nine-one-one? ... They're killing him ... nine-one-one?"
She was protected by her whispers and the black of the night,
was awakened from her single bench, and she continued counting
the rhythm of the ring-leader's shining army boot,
counting each kick, a note in the punching-bag
of his body as he could not call for help, no voice in his lungs,
already punctured by the second blow.

Austin Clarke

MAMMY-MAMMY-Mammy! Take this plea of love
and blood even from the reddened lips in a face
of black shoe polish, recite the confidence in his minstrel:
"The sun shines east, the sun shines west, I know
where the sun shines best, and I'll walk a million miles
for one of your smiles, my Mammy."

Where The Sun Shines Best

THEY KICKED the witness too into silence, and sent her on
her way, back to the home at Queen and Jarvis, lingering
over to confirm a philosophy: hear, see and speak
nothing about this little misunderstanding. The sun wiped clean
the black coarse metal of the unworkable cannon, and sprinkled
the water of its rays on the glass of the Armouries now washed
in glory; and the three soldiers, not freshened by the
    morning sun,
passed their hands over their faces, and erased
her evidence. She was too scared to talk. They kicked
the witness into silence, the sun rising before its time;
and they wiped their three palms across the blackboard
of their narrative; pulled the jackets of their uniform straight,
and walked in single file matching their report,
corroborating the facts, each word in place, just as the glass
at the entrance of the Armouries reflected the shine in
    their boots,
and the blood in their well-trained bodies; for they had kicked
the witness into silence, and had killed
the homeless man one kick later.

Austin Clarke

O, MAMMY, Mammy-Mammy-Mammy!
Will you walk that mile with me that sees two rivulets of water
cleanse my body at this mourning-telling sun of day
when the tears dribble down your cheeks like a harvester
in a field of poppies? Or corn? Or sugar cane?

WE HAVE killed the woman into silence; and the homeless man
who knew words and used them well, editing the torment
of others' prose, is silenced, too.

Austin Clarke

AND YOU are left alone, fumbling with the cord knotted
round truth and stupidity and loyalty, thick as the dust
you will breathe in Kandahar, if you get there still, to carry
out the killing ordered by war, and patriotism;
witnesses are absent, and there's no "bloody Book of Law,"
a page of calculus, perhaps, to complicate the way
you see things, and camels, and humans,
picked out in your sights.

About The Author

CULMINATING WITH the international success of *The Polished Hoe* in 2002, Austin Clarke has published ten novels, six short-story collections, and three memoirs in the United States, England, Canada, Australia, and Holland since 1964. *Storm of Fortune*, the second novel in his Toronto Trilogy about the lives of Barbadian immigrants, was shortlisted for the Governor General's Award in 1973. *The Origin of Waves* won the Rogers Communications Writers' Development Trust Prize for Fiction in 1997. In 1999 his ninth novel, *The Question*, was shortlisted for the Governor General's Award. In 2003 he had a private audience with Queen Elisabeth in honour of his Commonwealth Prize for his tenth novel, *The Polished Hoe*. In 1992 Austin Clarke was honored with a Toronto Arts Award for Lifetime Achievement in Literature. In 1997, Frontier College in Toronto also granted him a Lifetime Achievement Award. In 1998 he was invested with the Order of Canada, and since then he has received four honorary doctorates. In 1999 he received the Martin Luther King Junior Award for Excellence in Writing. In 2012, he won the $10,000 Harbourfront Award. Among his other achievements: Winner of the 2002 Giller Prize and co-winner of the 2003 Trillium Book Award for *The Polished Hoe*.

MARQUIS

Québec, Canada

Printed on Enviro 100% post-consumer EcoLogo certified paper,
processed chlorine free and manufactured using biogas energy.

100%   PERMANENT